World Stage Press
Verse from the Village

CAN'T NO WOMAN,
WOMAN LIKE ME

CAN'T NO WOMAN
WOMAN LIKE ME

POEMS BY JESSICA D. GALLION

World Stage Press
Verse from the Village

World Stage Press
Verse from the Village

Layout Design by Nadia Hunter Bey
Cover Design by Undeniable Ink
Cover Photo by Camari Carter

LAISSEZ LES BONS TEMPS ROULER!

French; Let the good times roll.
In Creole: Look out now, stuff's 'bout ta get real.
So, *laissez les bons temps rouler!*

Now, that Creole I'm referring to is a group risin' up out of Louisiana —
with all historical implications intact: fiercely family, lovin', cookin', and
laughin'. The women are fiercely beautiful, fiercely pretty — despite
anyone's opinion. You can't tell a 'French woman' she ain't 'Fire'... and
even her 'Flaws' will consume you in her 'woman fire.' At least that's the
rumor. This woman, this poet, is first that fiery Creole woman. She puts
all rumors to rest with naked truth-telling stories that ascend from the
very marrow of her bones and heart.

When she started this journey, her pen, like a match, would very
compliantly set fire to paper... albeit a small fire, there was still some heat.
But now, her pen has evolved to blowtorch status; and as this publication
approaches press, I am honored to watch her pen develop into a flame-
throwing weapon, defending all that would attempt to assault her or
anything and anyone she loves... or has loved! As love defends, so she
defends.

She is the winner of Ieshya Parker's fourth annual Women's Size it Up
Poetry Slam. Timid, determined, scared, and self-convinced she would
not win, Jessica captured the audience before they knew what hit 'em.
Being one of three competition judges (along with poets John 'Fly Poet'
Hensley and Jaha Zainabu), I had the distinct honor of witnessing this new
light in a sea of knowing women all come from hard stories and
descendants of strong raised fists in Black rhythm. They were all setting
some kind of fire on stage, but Jessica... carried her fire in the pockets of
her ragged bleached blue jeans fit tightly around them woman thighs.
That female, her dogged determination to get her story told without
reserve. And that she did. Amazed at her soft Southern voice, Creole-
laced, with an accent intonation only known in Creole culture, she
mystically and succinctly, in barefoot fashion, as if moving like Juju
through a misty forest of low riding tree branches dripping with Spanish

moss, came up from da Bayou and seduced the two story room without fanfare, without force.

Now, in her first book of fire, she dares place at your feet, a woman's journey through life's triumphs, struggles, defeats, and victories. As a single mother, not uncommon in the world we live in today, she rises like a phoenix to expose the truth of a woman with a pen as her fiery sword, setting afire the chaff to expose the reality of living day-to-day with the vehement love that quiets all doubt and question.

Her hope is that you get some goodness to help carry you through, finding some common ground in persevering. Although these writings are from a female perspective, there's no question that the men who dare embrace these writings will be seduced and captured by this consuming flame.

"Can't No Woman, Woman Like Me"

will provide a refuge in disrobed mystery and questions. As Jessica has picked-up the handle YELLAWOMAN in the Los Angeles Poetry community, she has become that soft voice of surety in the winning of the daily push to survive the onslaught of demands in everyday living. She is the loving power of woman—daughter, mother, lover, friend and poet. The doors are open, welcoming you with open arms, old-fashioned Southern hospitality, and the good cooking up of the words of the 'YELLAWOMAN Warrior Bird Poet'. LAISSEZ LES BONS TEMPS ROULER!

Reverdia, 'da River Woman,' Poet, Los Angeles

For Jayla... you will never be what they say you are

Table of Contents

GUMBO

EH, LA BAS !

BAY LEAF

COMME CI COMME CA

FLEUR - DE - LIS

LAGNIAPPE

JessLight

The Prophecy Of Her Woman
Holy Altered In silence
Meditation
Between Heart Conversations Oracled in rebel Birthmarks
She
She know
Be Mothers Mothers' Mother's After Garment
Swollen Womb Full Moon
She the Ceremony Of Stretch Mark Rebellion in Skin
Yella Woman
Louisiana New Orleans
Code Noir Socialized In The Congo Square Of Her Stance
She Here
Drum In Chest
Strings In Throat
Percussion Vocals
Her Music
Her Fight
Her Call and Response to Survive
Scribe the Lexicon of Her Creole
Summoned in the Pigment of Stolen Instruments Colonized in
Religion
French/Spanish Acculturation say
Make Afrika Hard to Hear
Hard to See
Her

How She Black Magic Purification Spells
Ink Dance Sacred Rituals Into The Pores of Sacrificed Trees
Drum Sound Converse Village Tongue Hidden Beneath Guided
Breath
Her Steps
Ancestor Songs Chanting Sankofa Hymns
Mother Spirit Say
She Be Healing Wounds
Domesticated in the Numbness of Mirror Work
The Affirmation of Her
In The Affirmation of Book
Proverbs of Medicine Women Seance in "Cant' No Woman
Woman Like Me"
The Voodoo of Her Presence Possess Her Wrist
Empower Her Significance to Transmit the Nakedness
of Her Folklore
She Invoke Dream Catchers
Transfuse Creation
Roots Rebirthed in Seed-JayBird
An Offering
Diction Delivered in Prayer
Her Woman
A Lifeline——————to You
In Word
"Word"

Eternal Mind

"We wear hula hoops in our ears so that we no longer have to jump through them, for we are now certain of our destination"
-Melanie S. Luja

CAN'T NO WOMAN,
WOMAN LIKE ME

gumbo

A thick soup/stew prepared from a roux base with meat, seafood, and filé served with rice. Depending on what part of Louisiana you are from, the roux may be darker or lighter. A tasty pot of a little bit of everything; not for everyone.

Standing Naked in Front of Amiri Baraka

Who you be?
Yella woman
This body has me all twisted
Goodly breasted
Belly birthin' beast in fire

Who you be?
What dirt they blow you from?
What Louisiana plantation porch shade yo' great gramma high yella
house nigga skin from the field?

Yella woman
Hair wrap and legs wrap 'roun massuh
Create linage
Whip neva touch yo' skin

What you know 'bout hurtin?
Stop yo' cryin'
Stop drownin' in yo' sorrow
Jump up and swim in sun

I see you shining yella woman
Who threw you in darkness?
Who stole yo' stars?
Who you be?
Tell me

Recipe Me

"Laissez les bons temps rouler!"
May I play for you a brass band jam
As we walk these streets of Bourbon, whiskey and good times
Let them roll
Ushered in to this life with purple, green and gold parasols
White hankies
Mardi Gras kings and queens dancing the alligator
I am marching 2nd line style with my ancestors

A freckled phoenix formed from generations of free slaves, mulatto and
quadroons strength
Cane River, Natchitoches folk
French breaded and Po'boy'd

Celebrating us don't make you us
Beads hang round my neck like gold chains
Shameless status
Proud to say we had slaves and have been slaves
Plantations still haunt us
Rice and Riches
Gumbo affection
Catholic tradition
Porch swinging
Tea sipping
Boy it's sweet

May I offer you a plate of knowledge Cher
Acknowledge me French
Consider me Spanish
Say you,
Black be me but my true color is love
Native to this land and every other
Not all things came free brother
Don't smother my culture because you too chicken to dig into the roots
My skin
My savory blend be forced
Marked yet untraceable

As I do a rain dance in Congo Square
With hair wraps and feathers on my feet
I welcome the ancestors with strong hips
Birthing life as I was born unto thee

Different walks two stepped and Zydeco'd me into life
Told me to save the past in present
Draped in fair skin
Tabasco running through my veins
Don't brown paper bag me my rights

I am jambalaya birthed from Andouille and faith
Don't ask who made me,
just say "Bless the cook."

LA to LA

Really couldn't tell you where I began
Stood on a front porch of a home not my own
Death knocked 3 times
We had to say goodbye
No more daddy or sister or grandpa
No more wooden floors or cast-iron skillets
No more braided fishtails and car rides
Just heartache
No familiar face

I was five and my nephew three
Not quite sure what we needed but Los Angeles wasn't it
I wanted to go home

I had the bayou blues
Moss trees
Swamp dreams
Crawfish and red beans
This was nothing savory
This city left a bad taste in my mouth
Tony Chachere's couldn't even help me out
It was loud and constant
Sirens and helicopters
Kids having more fun than I ever could here

Not knowing or understanding what was peace
Couldn't sleep knowing unhappy was taking over me
On that porch,
both worlds colliding inside me
leaving no room for what I was
only for what was to come
Louisiana was where I belonged,
but Los Angeles became home

Double Dutch

They wouldn't let me play
Yesterday was different
We laughed, traded a peanut butter sandwich for a Thermos of gumbo
Capri Suns and Juicy Juice
Double Dutched with a friendship rope
Made up dances and braided each other's hair
Toothbrush and Pro-Styled slicked down edges
I only needed more water
Rode bikes and skated passed the cute boy's house
A liquor store run for penny candy, nawlatas and bags of chips
I paid for everything and more
We played until porch lights flickered and our mamas called us home

But today,
Today I wasn't a part of, or a reason for their budding sisterhood
nor would I reap the fruit of it
My hair was too long today
My skin, too fair to be seen standing next to theirs
My tomboyish swag was too rough to be one of the girls
Today, I was alone
No one cared if I cried or what new dance moves I brought
Today I was a threat

"You think you all dat", they said
Funny how I felt all of nothing
I wanted to play and they was being mean
I didn't understand why on the same porch we did each other's hair,
they told me I could not come near

Rejected
I still stood there
Hoping the sadness that showed on my face would be enough for my
"friends" to just stop
Reconsider
But it didn't, they didn't
Why didn't I walk away?

Why did I stand there and allow them to hurt me more?
It's like the longer I stood there with my light skin, long hair, and tomboyish swag
The more ammo I gave them to send me running home crying
And I did
I cried and ran
And they laughed and chased me
Chased me like a mob running a witch out of town
I kept running

Alone
Defeated
I gazed over my skin wondering what was wrong with vanilla
I didn't care that they were caramel, butterscotch or chocolate
I have all these flavors in my family and we were a big ole sundae
Full of sweetness
Why don't they like ice cream?
I guess my 31 flavors were too much for their selective palates
I couldn't help that I had and liked variety
I was raised that way

Didn't matter if I was black
My black wasn't their black
I was just a white girl trying to be black
And I must have been out-blacking them because they were trying to remind me I was white
Never used those terms to describe my "friends", let alone anyone else
But today, I was all of that and nothin' else

Oxfords

Brave mulatto girl
Walks in her truth knowing her
White is her Black too

Love Roux

Barefoot and banging pots
Flaming cast iron greased to perfection
Hoping to make a meal of love
Adding:
1 pinch of salty tears
2 handfuls of hope
3 cans of affection
4 teaspoons of garlic truth
1 tablespoon of a sautéed embrace
And 2 cups of finely chopped pride
Smothered down to an orgasmic bite so satisfying you would be happy
to call it your last meal

Teacake's Love

I ain't neva been cared fo' befo'
'Least not by no man
Neva had no man touch me in no gentle way
Look at me and smile
Like he got a piece of sunshine stuck in his teeth
Like God made me just for him and can't nobody else make him feel like
dat

See I've always known mama's touch
Mama's cookin
Mama's huggin and bedtime stories and "booboo" kisses
Yeah,
She make everything all right,
All the time

Ain't had no man 'round my parts making me feel all special
See daddy been gone
Jesus called him home looooong time ago and before I would ever really
know his love, I had to say goodbye to his love
Sound like an ongoing trend if you ask me
Soon as I thought I had some love, it was time to say goodbye

But here you come,
Done made me feel like I could be special
Like somebody's very own piece of heaven
Like I was an angel or something
And even if it was only for a little bit,
I started coming up with stories 'bout yo' love
Wanting to feel yo' love
Have yo' love wrap me up like daddy's arms
Yo' lips whistling sweet things and calling me sweet names
I ain't never been somebody's "baby" befo'
Yeah,
But you done changed things

Natural Disaster "Single Mother"

It has been raining...
New Orleans style
For years, unsure how to pack
 Just like a tourist, I get caught in it with tank tops and flip-flops

Wet, cold, frustrated and hoping this isn't the next big hurricane
Wanting desperately to leave and get somewhere safe
But secretly hoping it only last for a little while so I can enjoy the
sunshine before I close my eyes

Sticky

Grip my hips and I can tell you it's honey
Submerge excited palms into pot
Let golden sticky coat brown sugar fingers
Bees are envious of the thick treasure you've had the pleasure to roam
What this comb provides makes allergy prone kings Benadryl for a feel
Be nectar robber turned beekeeper
Just keep her buzzing, flowing and dripping

Production happens seasonally but you can indulge more than
occasionally
Freely spread this on your breakfast for sweetness
Add me to your tea during sickness
And sop me up with a biscuit
The hive never runs dry
Try me and watch me boost your dopamine
Produce a surge of energy
My hips can cure anything... Naturally

Beaucoup

Love makes me fat
I become one with pots and pans
Plates and forks
Obesity is served
Love overload

It domesticates me
Four burners running simultaneously is the only fire present
Fetching your dinner
Baking your dessert
Never anytime to chew the pain
I swallow disappointment whole

Swollen in love
Wobbling in suppressed feelings
Too plump to feel tasty enough to be your midnight snack
Why is love so decadent?
So heavy?

Eh, La Bas!

Hey! Over There!
(Call and Response)

Who Run The World

Barefoot kitchen conversations about how the world turns as we
command balance of our own globes on index fingertips pointing
toward the Most High
We women was left to our own devices as the men stood tribal-style,
strategizing their next move as their best move in cool breezes so the
universe knew they wasn't playing

Cigars and brandy became peasant pleasantries as poets pushed pen in
verbal libation creating sage smoke visions
Our world was safe as 4 kings sat guard in front of the castle while 4
princesses slept and 6 queens confessed their campaign strategies to love
first...whomever they choose at that time
14 souls united under solar return energies and seeds were sown in
portals we haven't even begun to hop

Rainbow black
Melanin messages spread 'cross faces and souls as we divulged
motherhood/village secrets and "Hell naw you ain't crazy" healing
All of us turned inside out as tears fell and laughs elevated
Elder sat tallest as locs laid on lap in place of her hands
Bearing gifts
10 fingers laid on us as jewels dropped making all of our crowns heavier

We cleansed chakras last night
We were black moon and stars
Fire and rain
We held earth in our wombs
In our wounds

Our own globes spinning on index fingertips simultaneously
Knowing that we were not alone
We share the same moans and groans
Highs and lows
And our kings
Stayed up front,
Strapped head to toe with verbal ammunition and paws for anyone who
wanted some

40

Never was a question
Never bothered us like they knew we had business to attend to
So they waited
Understanding that whatever we were up to was designed to hold them
up too

good Hair

My princess sits and flips through hair magazines
Pretty must hurt because she feels the need to change
Desperately looking for a style that fits, but no one looks like her
Covers and pictures in-between are
Pale-skinned
Blonde-haired
Blue-eyed
Curling ironed-curls,
Bleached waves and tousled strands

No trace of this olive-toned
Sun kissed-coated
Creole caramel girl's wild curlicue, untamed mane
With two luscious ponytails and a flower dress

She teases gravity
This mixed chick with natural pecan colored curls is searching for herself
Flipping page by page with antsy fingers
Excited for the moment she is able to point and say " Oooh mama I want this!"
No such luck

I wonder if she knows that she is special?
That can't no one reflect her but her
Will she understand she is walking art?
Unexpected perfected brush strokes
Never to be framed or hung in homes
But adored from afar and free to roam beyond the borders of a magazine

Princesses' tresses are to be emulated
They will buy bundles and packs of you
Make you an array of colors, too
That curly, wavy, threadlike tapestry, naturally curves and bends
Can be combed, picked , straightened, braided and celebrated
Don't you know they are envious of you
Desperately want to be like you
You, my dear, are the blueprint with no recipe
They try hard to recreate you
Failing miserably every time

Your whirls and twirls were made for beach fronts and speed boats
Spring breezes and summer sundown's
Understand you will bathe in envious stares and "Ooo girl can I touch your hair?!"
Throw away your ponytail holders, ribbons and bows
Let go of the restrictions
Continue showing up glowing
Hair bouncing
Energy shining
Curls smelling of coconut oil and lavender
20 inches of B natural and 100% You
All day
Everyday
Women will point and say,
"I wish I had her hair"

I hope she sees everything they see
A curlicued, untamed and free princess,
too good for the pages of what oughta be

A Sinner's Plea

I broke my rosary beads, tell me you don't hate me

My hands and knees are black and blue from kneeling and bending at

candles and statues

Tell me you hear my cry

My bible has tear stained pages that smell of frankincense and myrrh

Fingertips burned with sage, yet everything I touch seems to go up in

smoke

Blessings on the horizon seem so intangible when you feel distant

God, are you listening

How much heart do you think I have?

Must I bathe in holy water to get a prayer answered?

I was baptized every Easter

Drank your blood every Sunday

Played with salvation every weekend yet this host is empty

Much like my pockets after tithing

Tell me You do house calls

Help me raise my children

I am failing Father

My fingers have melted into everlasting prayer hands

Leaving molds for my children's children's children to reference you

Begging hands now remain closed

There is nothing for me to receive here

Did I upset you?

I know I should have listened, but I couldn't hear you while he was

beating me

You are hard to see during defeat

A closed fist to the face seems to make more noise than hands clinched to

the Good Book any day

Where were you when we had nothing to eat?

Nowhere to sleep?

Was I not hungry enough?

Obedient enough and still enough?

Had things not gotten real enough?

Have I not forgiven me enough?

With hands molded shut I beg you,

Use me Lord, heal me Lord

I have had enough

No Animal

Black Man ain't no animal
Just because you hunt, shoot, and kill him for sport
Don't mean you get to trophy his head on precinct walls
Interesting how he never becomes endangered
Funny how he survives after years and years of buying, selling, trading
and killing him off

Black Man ain't no animal
And although he is a rare bird,
Don't mean you get to strategically pluck and clip his wings with a full
clip as we watch a clip of it on social media
See he be ebony phoenix
Rising despite gun smoke
Soaring high above expectations with every degree
Every black owned business
Every sacred marriage
Every son and daughter that knows him and every community that
depends on him for their very existence
I'm telling you,
He ain't no animal

Because if he was
He would have ripped yo' ass open long time ago
Sank his teeth in, dragged your lifeless body back into the cave
Devoured your ignorance and left your bones discarded for all to see
See,
He don't want none of yo' kind running though his veins
Never wants to become like the animals that treat him like prey

But since he is hunted,
He knows when to run
How to hide
Doing his best to dodge bullets
Traps and trick ropes just so he don't end up hanging from one
BLACK MAN AIN'T NO ANIMAL
Running don't make him no punk
He is breaking free from the cage they tried to put him in

He could never be tamed or trained
No matter how much you whip him,
The shape he is in will never be for your benefit
The day he turns animal, is the day,
The jungle falls

Anticipation

Damn he turns me on
Listening to him talk about his future sends chills down my spine
Hearing how he's planning on winning got me planning on sinning
And since I've been praying for him to win
Listening to him speak is like listening to God confirm He's been
listening to me and talking to him
I mean, who's not excited when they get what they want?

I want him to win
I want us to spend every moment chasing our dreams and creating big
things because we fly like that
I get Christmas morning wrapped up in his fly
Excited to tear off every bit of his surprise because I'm learning more and
more how stimulating anticipation is — aphrodisiac
My whole body becomes a deep pulsation when he talks that talk
I get peach bitten juicy when he walks that walk

He's out here trying to change lives y'all, and I wanna be front row
feeling indo high
Cloud surfing
Mother like nurturing
I be right hand in his plan and he ain't even gotta share the blueprint
because I've been designing and creating...
Architect be my middle name all while waiting for his last name to be on
my documents

I tell him "keep dreaming baby, keep doing your thing, keep talking that
talk and walking that walk
I'm right hand man beside you,
Cheering yo' name,
Praising God's name
Signing checks and checkin' off accomplishments"
We gonna win so big, won't nobody forget

Damn... body pulsating just thinking about it

Queen B

When nothing you say seems to come out right
Everything on the inside never gets understood
When you are left feeling like the villain of your own story
Told in tears, knowing you spoke the truth and all its ugly
When BITCH seems to be the other name on your birth certificate
when some think of you,
Speak of you or point at you...
Smile
Don't let it stop you from standing tall
Be that ruthless, truthful, villain of a BITCH they say you are
And with tears in your eyes tell them
"Fuck you and I loved you"

Nerve

You don't get to just fuck me anymore
I am more than backseats and dark rooms
Lights on when you feel bold enough to see me arched at the waist for
you
I am not just Heroine lipstick stains on glasses of Remy and Magnum
wrappers
2am phone calls post grinding at the club I wasn't invited to
"WYD" texts when you and her aren't cool

I can smell her through the phone
When you call me with 151 and arguments on your breath
Your "Come sit on my face" DM's are stimulating and nauseating
I know, to you, I'm sloppy seconds
You tell me to call you "Daddy"
Mine is dead and your daughter doesn't know you
This turns me off the minute you command me to do so
Please
Let's just stick to Mike
I heard a man hearing his name repeatedly out of a woman's moaning
voice and even in casual conversations gets his attention
Listen to me "come" saying your name

Mike,
I have come to the painful yet obvious conclusion that you are an idiot
No longer worth my time
My efforts
My orgasms
I'm taking them all back

Mike,
Honey,
I won't be cumming for you again anytime soon
You are free to go be "Daddy"
Go raise your daughter
The daughter you don't want to claim, much like me
Then maybe you'd learn to value a woman
Possibly understand the importance of feelings

When you see her heart broken, you will flash back to this face
When she leaps into your chest and wraps her arms around your neck,
much like I've done several times upon sight...
Then you will see the honor in being called "Daddy" and why it never
came off my tongue for you

Polished Trash

Who told you could walk away?
What makes you think you're in control?
I hold the cards
The pussy
The power
I run this shit

What makes you think you can leave?
I held your hand
Prayed Hail Mary's walking down the street
Anointed your head with Ruby Woo lipstick kisses because you were my king
I cooked red beans and rice for you

Who in the hell told you, you could leave?
I looked good just for you
Wore sexy strappy heels and tight skirts
Even wore Flower Bomb perfume for you
Placed it on the inside of both of my thighs in hopes you would come alive

How could you eva walk away?
French-tipped my toes and finger nails
Did away with the colors I wanted
Scratched your back and placed my pedicured feet against your chest
Hoping you wouldn't walk all over me

What makes you think you can leave me?
I waxed and stayed groomed for you
Shaved my legs and hid bleeding nicks from you
How dare you treat me, like touching me was a crime?

We Don't Live in Castles

He said:
Here, you can have them
I don't want these scars, never did.
Better yet
I'm not claiming them.

So, here
Go crazy
Go crazy for me so I can leave you
Let your crazy be a reflection of my ego
Remind me of me so I can no longer look at you
Same reason I don't own mirrors baby
Nobody has seen me in a long time
Not even me

Understand these scars are deep
You loving me whole-heartedly reminds me I'm a monster on the inside
And your beauty is too precious for my beast
I'm sorry but you could never love me to prince

No matter the elegant dress
The soft hands
The slow dance
I will always be a beast in a tux
Give up and if you don't I will
You have no idea what kind of wicked I feel
See I'm trying to spare you

Listen
Women don't listen
Your love
Sex
Support   ·
Your home cooking will never be enough if we never had it enough to
cherish it enough to wife you
We "wife" when we are ready to

And you will never know if it's really you because we will still cheat on
you and blame you
Apologize to you
But darling it's never you

It's me
It's we
It's us
"That's what men do"
Very true and untrue,
Depends on if you are in the presence of prince or beast
And you will never know until it's too late
Your love will be the one to get further than all others
And we will not be ready

It will all be too much for both of us
Jump on your white horse
You are too much princess and queen to ever be damsel in distress
Ride off into the sunset with your heart and beauty still in tact
Because there is no victory in trying save a man who doesn't want saving

Voice

He said, "Take care of that pretty voice"
I didn't know what he meant
Does he know I frighten people with this voice?
Run people off with this voice?
I'm not your 24-hour affirmation spokeswoman
Nothing lovely I speak
At times failures seem to rest at the tip of my tongue
No wonder dreams tend to crumble and die when I speak
I small talk me

Still learning how to hone this voice
Own it
Speak it victory
Make your sons man up with this voice
Let little boys fall to the wayside with this voice
Make people step up
I'm saving lives with this voice

My message ain't pretty
Struggle ain't pretty
Failure ain't pretty
I am fragile and I ain't
Sit up straight when I talk to you
I told you, you were a king,
Believe it
I spoke better things for you
My voice was too much mirror
Don't ever say it's pretty
It's real
Body smooth and flexible, real
God gave me breath so I'm real
Laughter and faith... is real

I told you, my voice is not for your comfort...it's for your growth

Written Testimony

With pen in hand
My lips are sealed
Not saying a thing
I write it down so it's truth
Bible
God has spoken
-shut up

Bay Leaf

A bitter seasoning leaving behind a sharp and pungent taste.
Used to communicate the spirit of prophecy and poetry.
Commonly put under pillows at night to gain inspiration
through dreams and its intoxicating properties are
associated with prophetic and poetic inspiration.

Battered Canvas

His abuse was like art.
With every stroke of his hand, he created a monster
Trying to find beauty in the chaos he created,
I stand in the mirror everyday
Searching for his inspiration

BD

When he choked me I laughed
Not sure which one of us was crazy
I wasn't scared of him
Five fingers became noose around my neck
I dangled in front of him
He was my first everything
Nothing was ok with anything
Nothing Christian Grey about his grab
I still had enough breath in me to smile though
Pageant style
Miss America crowned

And this wasn't his first time
Senior year of high school was stressful that way
This 6'1"
Rock solid, firearm
Big little boy of a man, prison rage mutated
Chest and arms became too big to ever be gentle giant
And his head grew bigger than the one he head butted me with a month
before
Hulk-like man-beast tried to shatter my voice
My laughter pushed already tampered buttons
Prison PTSD, look a lot like soldiers
We was on the yard
I mean on the field
But I was up against his living room door, in love and laughing
My breast, smashed against his heart
That green monster pushed me and I flew
I never landed
Silly man tried to take my breath
...he simply made me laugh

Baby

I was keeping my baby
18...I'm somebody's mama now
I was grown

No longer 17 and lost
Still very unsure
Still learning these curves, unsure
Unemployed, unsure
Him, in and out of jail, unsure
But... I knew

Long before he gave me a diaper bag full of apologies, money, bottles
and ego
Never his heart
I knew I wasn't having no abortion... Merry Christmas

I knew before he was ok with it
Told him to wrap his head around being a father
Here or not, he was

I just graduated high school
Book smart, street smart, and my mama ain't neva been no fool
So I knew,
I was 18...and I was keeping my baby

Love Floats

With tears in my eyes, I asked him
"Who is she?"
Days, and sometimes weeks, of ignoring her calls were ringing loud
Her voicemails sounded far beyond friend
Her "I love you" and "Call me back, I miss you," sound very attached
I know that attachment
Almost 2 years and a pregnant belly later
Lord knows, I know
So tell me,
Who the fuck is she?

Between his head shaking and eye rolling, he managed to shout innocent
pleas
"Where is this coming from?"
"What are you talking about?"
"Man, get outta here!" and
"I don't have time for this shit."
They flew from his mouth so defensively
Like me wanting to know who could possibly love him more than me,
was a blow to his character

I didn't care how mad he got
I had two hearts in me and they both were breaking
And to me,
That Rock, Paper, Scissored any anger he felt during my Q&A

"Are you fucking her?"
"Does she know about me?"
"She know you got a baby on the way?"
Questions sounded like they were about her
Really they were reminders for to him to see what he was throwing
away

His silence was equivalent to guilty
I wanted him to say he was sorry
I wanted him to tell me she was nobody

But I knew,
And he knew I knew
His silence and my tears flooded the room
We both drowned in truth
My baby was the only one that survived

No Balloons

He had his new girlfriend pick him up from the hospital the morning after I had given birth to our daughter

It was my birthday

Worth It

I wish I could tell you that I'm ok
That I'm open to experiencing what is really meant for me
Start acting like God has a plan for me and this ain't the end of me
I wish my faith was where it used to be
And in the same breath,
I know that I'm blessed...
Just stressed

But I have thought about would it might be like
You know
To let you in
And how I might start smiling again
Ear to ear
That "I don't know him just yet but he can get it" grin

Imagining possibilities:
Like us becoming poetry
Swapping war stories of "who did it?" and "how could they ever do you
like that?"
Long distance desires
"Good morning, beautiful" texts
And phone sex
But no nude flicks

We are poets`
I'd much rather feel every syllable as you haiku my eardrum
Giving me eargasms as I fantasize about your beard grazing my thighs
as you recite Lord Byron on my clitoris
Exhaling
Screaming your name like it was hallelujah

I wish I could tell you I was open

I honestly no longer know how to be
Unsure if I ever want someone to get know me this well
Again
Uncomfortable with letting someone hold me because I have been held

with empty hands
Willing to give nothing up for me
I don't know if I'm ready for that
Again

I wish I could tell you I was open,
Maybe I am, deep inside
I'd like to think that you could help pull me out but I'm scared
Not every woman is rescued and shown how to really be loved directly
after having her heart thrown away
Not every woman is treated like treasure after being tossed out like
polished trash
Held in humble hands and kissed with hallelujah breath
And I'm not looking for you to
It's all on me
I just wish I was open to feeling like a blessing

Black Roses

She smells of love
The stench of trying after all has left is pungent like bleach
Scrubbing soiled carpets and souls spotless after arguments turned crime
scene
Clean fingernails never meant clean slate

A fragrant aura of midnight blue
Like bags under tired eyes
I bet there are traces of blood in her tears
Fresh wounds meeting alcohol-dipped fingers always made his support
burn
Causing her tears and wiping them never allowed code blue remedies
Hero syndrome never manifests harmless rescue

How could he fall for her again
Like causing her to hit rock bottom wasn't a form of worship
With hands to the sky,
Begging him
Begging God
She made him a God you know, biblical
She was King James holy
Dead Sea Scrolls mystery
10 Commandments obedient
Baptismal commitment, and he was too busy for church

Her love stunk of dedication
Pushing strategically on brick walls made her strong for no reason
He never caved in
Don't be foolish girl
He will never give in

Filthy from heartbreaks torture and Kama Sutra's massaging oil,
He always played dirty
Bending truth
Flexible in omitting
After all, he was never all in
Whispering sweet nothings

He never shared his secrets
She listened with loving ears
Smelling of understanding,
A scent he never cared to call home

Fuckboy Flowers

Never have I been just the pretty petals on a rose
I'm the thorns, too
Don't come in my garden unless you are ready for pleasure and pain

The most beautiful sought out flower of them all
Never request a dozen if you aren't ready to do the work for each one
Know your limits...
                  and go buy some damn carnations

Ghost Writer

I have turned my pen over to you
When ink mixes with tears
Our history is written
My history
You will be long gone
We will be long gone before these poems hit ears that have never heard
of us

This is my legacy
Trying too hard
8 months after the break up too hard
Cooking for you too hard
Standing by your side, heels and skirts, arm candy too hard
Compromising my health
Xanax and therapy too hard
Sharing my family still
Holidays and birthdays still
My thoughts
Sleeping on the very couch that smells of us still
Inhaling us still
Hosting this hazardous energy
And still,
You never stop giving me poems
Never stopping yourself in your tracks and saying "This is enough"
No,
I'm crazy again
Over reacting again
Causing you strife
I am your downfall again
The reason for your sage spray again
"I rebuke thee demon"
Causing you grief again

I have given you my pen
This love will make me the Taylor Swift of poetry
Manuscripts of heartbreak
"We used to be mad love, you made a really deep cut

Now we got Bad Blood"
I too will make millions off your foolishness
What woman hasn't had her heartbroken
What woman doesn't get to the point where she Marvin Gaye throws up her hands and hollers
What woman doesn't get to the point where her God is all that matters

You 9/11'd me
Crashed your insecurities into my brick house and burned my soul to the ground
Dreams became casualties
Paranoia and mayhem broke loose in me
You fucking terrorist
How dare you come on free soil and create fear
How dare you make everyone watch me with "What hell is she go do" eyes?
How dare you walk away like rebuilding ain't because of you?
How dare you ask to assist in the rebuilding?
The one that broke you CANNOT fix you

But I can write poems, and I will

Tasting Tears

I know those tears,
Trust me
I've felt that blow to your chest
Like you've been hit by a car
Left for dead

I know those tears,
Trust me
That knot in your throat
All the words you wish you said instead
It's thick ain't it?

I know those tears
They fall like the walls around your heart when you let him in
When he kinda did the same
Trust me,
I know
Mad at yourself
Disappointed
Staring in the mirror, hoping to see him appear behind you
But he's not there
I know those tears
I've had those same fears

I also know love
Love can be the most wonderful
Terrifying
Fantastic
Captivating
Marvelously painful thing you may ever feel
And if it ever leaves, continue to be beautiful.
Love yourself harder
You are still worthy of all things God has promised...
Trust me, I know

Missing Him

It's in my bones
I lay with it
The tears
The memories
The regret
Our story plays over in my head like old movies
From the first hesitant kiss to the last kiss on the cheek

Tears caress that same cheek much like his lips
The tears fell harder
My bones started hurting
Making it impossible to walk
To stand tall
To move in grace
Walk in love
Our love had become like arthritis
Crippling
I was missing him
And my bones didn't care

Heartbreak...Venti

Looking forward to coffee not tasting like you
Ice cream not smelling like you
This couch we sat on for almost a year,
Not feeling like your arms

I sleep there,
On that couch,
The one that holds tears
Laughter
Sex and the City marathons
Memories of foot rubs and home cooked meals
Poetry
On paper and our hearts
The ones that we shared and the ones we kept for ourselves

I look forward to not breaking down every 5 minutes
But smiling at the woman that stands after the heartbreak
I don't know if your arms would ever stop feeling like home, but I hope I
will always be welcomed

For Closure

You felt claustrophobic in what I called home
These arms and legs became jail cell residency
Wanting to escape this brick house
Limbs now heavy as bricks
We suffocated playing house

Mud and light molded this frame
I was sanctuary and solid
Now, an eye soar, broken hedges, and squeaky floorboards
Rubble and less secure
Unable to recognize my hands

I tried landscaping
Eyes provided waterfalls for hopes and dreams
Seeds of negativity sown
Blooming insecurities and thorn bushes
Roses never grew
Renovating this beautiful cottage to please squatters
Someone, nail a "No Trespassing" sign on my heart

Baewatch

I wish he would just cry already
Stop fighting the tides inside
His beauty
His beast
Lifejacket himself in pep talks and meditation
Coast with the currant
Break free from self-loathing anchors
Let the tsunami come so I could lifeguard his soul
Rescue him with mouth to mouth confessions
Tell him I've always been here to ride the waves from his eyes...
I sea him

Perfectly Fine Human

Gratitude is best served with a closed mouth
Tape placed tell over my lips like some form of foreplay
He wanted me quiet
I wish I could be silent
Smother the screams rising in me behind the obedience

I regret my woman
Closed thighs
I'm selective in choosing
Knowing they are gates to life
To love

But I adored him
This man
Broken yet perfectly structured mosaic human
I broke free
Razor blade tongue slices tape
Bloody truths uttered in healing dialect
Thighs open to life
To love
Calling him home with my lips

Comme Ci Comme Ca

(Like this like that; Neither good nor bad)

Fire and Flaws

Doubt sometimes is an inferno

Flames surround this body of water

Persistence is so fluid but it's drying me up

Acceptance is the bridge I flow under

How I wish these flames would engulf acceptance

Let it burn all doubt and just let me flow...

Freely

Liberate me and watch me flood the minds of these fools

Thirsty hotheads

Quench the nation

They have been dehydrated for ages...

Until my fire

Until my flaws

Closet Freak

You closet me in shame
My thick frame leaves you questioning who's to blame on why you enjoy
climaxing and saying my name
Too bad you hide the beauty of us
All of who you really are stays in darkness
Every one of your desires is put up on hangers
Beautifully displayed and arranged
Color coordinated, textured pleasures integrated

I stand
Endlessly frustrated, but ever so patient, ready for play
My majestic radiates through key hole and cracks in the not so tightly
sealed door you so desperately try to keep closed
How hasty of me to think you kept me stored in this Pandora's box for
selfish play
When all the while,
You've been so insecure, that you hide me

Afraid of what peers may say, you played me to the left day after day
I took it, because we weren't together anyway
Holding on to false promises of "maybe"
And phrases that began with "when WE"
As if WE could ever be anything outside of these sheets

Crazy how your days are filled with thin girl cliques and weave infused
chicks
And all this time, I thought what you liked was my natural curls and
curvy hips
I'm puzzled trying to piece together "this"
You share things with me so sweet and intimate
You caress and grope every area that seems stressed
Blessed are these exchanges
Yet amongst your boys you quickly fall into the phrase of "boys will be
boys"
And dem boys only play with the popular toys
Despite what they thought, they heard of how you prefer her, her and
her

It's me you long for, I'm the one who's always left you wanting more

Surely closets hold skeletons and secrets
I guess you planned on keeping this love a graveyard mystic

Deep Treatments

Twirling fingers in my thoughts
Careful to not tangle self in my mess
Palms be conditioner to this dry mane
Strokes of tea tree electrify my pores
Love intertwined in tousled locs
Only you can comb through the chaos of these crimson strands
Energy never bland
I am the fall down the rabbit hole
Eyes are a wonderland
Get lost
Tightly grip these fire antennas
They are here for your entertainment
Just don't blame me for your burns

9 to 5

Work your kisses down
Watch me clock'n on love
Slave in overtime for hugs…
The benefit package is better than drugs

Track No. 1

You are my favorite song
I put you on repeat
Everyone and everything else tuned out
You make me sing in the shower
Water drops fall like liquid lullabies
Making my back quiver from every adlib
I sleep in the serenade of you
Your music has changed me
I awake with a 2 step in my feet,
Choreographing our love to the beat

Star Fishing

I thank God I awoke being able to say your name...It tastes like stars

I promise I reached my hands to the blue sky in praise, when I speak of
you,
My mouth blows stardust, creating galaxies of you,
Of us

I tried catching stars last night
Tried grabbing that end-of-the-tunnel light from the sky
Wanted to see if I could shed some light on the subject of us
Wanted to see if God would let me borrow some of HE to fix WE
because only He can

Our light dims more and more with every fight, shedding less and less
potential for recovery
That heat we bring when angered words ring, makes wedding rings
seem so far away

How dare we make a mockery of a union
How dare we compare this darkness
To the radiant glare of 1
Our 1 and 1 never makes 2
Hell, we both odd...
Too odd to ever think about calling it even...
Misunderstanding has us feeling misunderstood by the 1 we need to
have overstood

I beg of you, act like you know my heart while we stand in our rightful
corners
When we fight till morning, please know you are not the only one
mourning

I promise, I tried catching stars last night

Art Works

Late nights and deep thoughts
I crave touches like I never been touched
Lavender hands soothe callus skin
Smooth and rough
Just like us
Best of both worlds at the same time
Time stands still as if we own this world
Whenever we are near
Pleasure and fear run rampant
My heart is at attention

He has painted moons in every black and white
No room for grey when he comes with an array of hues
Yellows and pinks and greens, and even his blues are true
Come,
Color me
Feel free to fill freely
Go outside the lines
I am blank canvas
Art me

April's Noel

Flickering blue lights surround us
Creating oceans with wave like conversation
The currents run deep
Thank goodness I can swim
Words create a mental mist
But misty I am not
Blue is the color of this union
The hue of my sight
Eyes brown and skin smooth
We connected under blue suede mistletoe
My shoes are stuck
Kiss me

Space Jam

The moon and stars belong to ours
And mars isn't too far so just stay right next me...
This is home
We can catch intergalactic love as we surf on shooting stars in Milky
Ways
I love you something like everyday
And by the way, I was never fake
I love you endlessly
Even if you aren't next to me
It's something I cannot control
My love is whole
Never half
Unless we talking about you
Because you are half of me
I would love to be half of you
You and I are cosmic, and it's obvious that we connect, like so far back,
we light years ahead of the now
They can't keep up
Gravity has made many casualties of love
But we survive,
We stand strong
Because we the Big Bang
Bang bang
You shot me down
Bang bang I hit the ground
And I float and levitate
The sky is begging for me
Come on let's elevate
Play
Swim in the bigger dipper
Pull triggers of stardust
While we busy making constellations
Baby, making generations
As we sit from our third eye view,
Baby, we higher than bird's eye news!!
We can rule this place
You and I

Stay by my side
Here, at home
Where the love is strong and the stars are warm

Listening Party

If these tunes weren't playing, I'd be lying here wishing I could tune out
I can't hum loud enough to cover up
the fuck up I'm doing on my cover of life
How I wish I could sing a new song
Repeat has been pressed for so long
I forget there were other tracks
Other options never seemed like an option when the fast-forward button
was stuck
A constant rewind on melodies allows memorized rhymes to flow
naturally...
You'da thought I was free styling

I'm just doing it again
My song's on again
Turn it up,
Time to destroy every effort on creating a new sound
Wearing last week's frown has me looking vintage with no value
I'm stuck on a single, forgetting I'm the album
The world is waiting for a new release, and I can't even find the volume

Boudoir Olympics

He made me do gymnastics on a mattress
Made my body pretzel in a mirror
Balancing on your beam defied gravity
You have some of the best floor work I have ever seen
I would sprint every time you called
And your backstroke created pools
Yeah, I remember you,
You always took home the gold

Fleur - De - Lis

is "**flower** of the **lily**." This symbol, depicting a stylized **lily** or lotus **flower**, has many meanings. Traditionally, it has been used to represent French royalty, and in that sense, it is said to signify perfection, light, and life.

Sunrise...

To Jessica:

Growing should be exciting not scary. Becoming amazing is the focus and the constant, not who or what made you grow. You can always be sure of you; you have the right to be happy and here, in this moment. Growth and self-development will always be a great addition to any relationship; and what is for you, will always be for you. Don't get attached to the idea of losing someone and everything falling apart, get attached to knowing that no matter who is here on your journey, they are not the reason. You are.
You are important, you are the focus, and you are the whole! Balance and keep self in mind.
You can't fall apart... You have to be strong in self to be strong in any relationship. Keep growing, keep finding your way and keep God and love first.
You got this!!
Love,

Me

Self-101

Learn to take a compliment woman
Stop laughing when they tell you you are beautiful
There is nothing funny about your glory
Take comfort in the fact that very few speak but they all watch
It's respect
Desire
Fear
Envy
Ignorance

Hold your head up
Put on your lipstick
And smile

Dead End Sessions

Come,
Sit down with me
Tell me your fears
Your "why I'm here's"
It's ok
You are not the first

I've sat in several passenger seats and listened
Encouraged
Held hands
Understood
Prayed

Men have unloaded their secrets
Their desires
Shamelessly
No yelling
Lips trembling as exhaustion ran from their eyes
Down their faces

I sat,
Watching
Listening
Smelling good enough to eat
Barefaced, freckled peace

Many have felt safe without explanation
Without question
They see my power
Trust it
Know I hold no punches
Straight shooting
No smoke
With a touch of "she gets it"

Home they call it
Therapy at midnight

Faith healing

I'm told I always know what say
I speak in metaphors
My poems,
I always have a poem,
Are the cure and the cause
The perfect description of symptoms along with a prescription
My hands are John Hopkins
Come,
Let me heal you
Restore you back to king
Laying hands as I wrap you in these arms
Sending you on your way until the next time you need me

Warrior Bird

Although she is a child,
She is a warrior
She holds, throws and dodges bricks and stones
The shit is heavy
She wakes up fighting and she is never tired
Every heartbeat is a possible heartbreak,
For her or me...
But no matter what, she keeps pushing
Bad days still result in straight A's
And for that, you keep pushing
I believe I've shown her that
I've shown her that no matter what,
I got her back and she would never experience love like that again

I've shown her that cloud 9 is above the ceiling and no one is going to
help you float
Baby please hear me,
You must elevate above
Shatter generational curses
You must realize that God carries us through tough times and because of
him
We can fly
Ascension in your queendom is necessary for your lineage
You MUST set the tone for yourself
And those to follow so they may be able to follow your reign!!

Baby, nothing happens on the ground
Even roots are underground
And what grows never stops just as it breaks through!!!
Bust down walls,
Use those stones and bricks to demolish that glass house of insecurities
Be more concrete in yourself
Others will recognize your strength
And even when they don't, you must know you can still do anything

No matter how tough the road gets,

Know you may face everything alone
And You just may have to save yourself!
Sometimes you are the rescue, the white horse and the damsel in distress
So be a BEAST, and NEVER let ANYONE tame you

Diamond in the Rough

I wasn't broken when you found me
You caught me while learning how to properly adjust my crown
So many jewels have been added, it weighs my head down
I see you feel the need to remind me during tough times
My tears are not a reflection of my inability to
Stand tall
I told you why I was hunched over
I stood before you flaws and all

Unfortunately, yes, I do still seek your approval
Even if you are by my side,
I still need to hear you say it
It needs to be truthful
Since I've met you,
Know you have added crystals too
You've managed to set me back all while making me push through
Overstand that your words, too, weigh heavily
They have the power to strengthen, or they can be weakening,
Damn near deadly

So be a source of good things
It feels good being able to recharge on your strength
I need that energy
Trying to keep a level head while elevating through each level
afraid isn't easy
But believe me
I'm actually taking it day
        by
                day

No matter what you think you see,
Recognize the queen inside of me
And although my crown may be tilted
Never underestimate the power within it
Understand that these jewels aren't Swarovski
This headpiece is not from Tiffany's

Every gem is unique
Placed strategically to balance chakras
Earned through hard work and defeat
I am a masterpiece completely incomplete
But I ROCK this shit because it's my legacy

War Paint

I put my make up on last
In the car
Between red lights
I never do it at home in the bathroom mirror
Like normal women

Too many tears to apply the mascara at home as I see myself in floor
length mirrors
The tiny rearview mirror is perfect
I can leave those thoughts behind me and see only my face

My freckles are my friends
I have many
I can count on them
They are always shining
My natural highlight

They help me forget about the too many outfits tried on and thrown
Getting dressed is a battle
A chore
Shaper and bra got everything snatched
Held together like I got it together
I've broken down at least three times

But in the car, none of that matters
I have committed to leaving and smiling
I always try smiling after combat
I dig through my makeup bag and pull out my biggest gun,
The boldest lipstick I can find
Today my lips won the war between self and self

Flying

Untuck your wings when mountains come crashing down
Do not resist flight because your eyes are filled with tears
Soar north, out of the valley where all the bones are buried
Do not grant breathing skeletons the privilege of making you feel
claustrophobic
'
Break free from shameful closets like coming out parties and fed up
secret lovers
Stretching your wings in new truth every time you find yourself falling
beck first into arguments
Lift your head to see what's in front of you
Simply a challenge,
Never the enemy

Flock in love
Sister-girl circle
Skelton slayers
Breathing connoisseurs
Align your queendom as you soar above the flames

Salvation

I cut my hair
It was the only thing left I could do
I couldn't cut my skin
Feared this shell of a woman I had become wouldn't stop bleeding
I wouldn't ask for help

I cut my hair
I couldn't cut off my stomach
Ate everything I could and swallowed pride
Became the exact thing I swore I'd never be for a man
Tear after tear
I am bloated with regret

I cut my hair
I didn't want to cut off my emotions
I brushed and combed, pulled and yanked my mind
Never could style it just right for you

I cut off my hair
It was the calm after the storm
I've thrived off the arguments, the laughs and the make-ups
But as the hair fell,
I knew smiles and peace were ahead of me

I cut off my hair because I no longer cared
What you thought
What they thought
What I think matters
I missed the me I was before you, so I cut off my hair

Morning Rituals

Magnolias on her breath when she woke
Stomped death every time her feet hit the floor
She inhaled defeat
Exhaled a bouquet of miracles
Losing wasn't kin to her
She bathed in rose water
Washed away sin in the most fragrant way
We all couldn't smell like God
Drenched in holy and dripping spirit,
The hands of prayerful ones quaked
She is what they had been praying for
A guardian that held the key to locked doors
And peace within
She is the one we aspired to be
It is in us
Mighty are those that climb off the damnation they ride everyday
Washing off the heartbreak worn on their faces
Gargling filth out of their voices

We too can smell of God,
We just have to stop bathing in the devil

Flaming Hope

She don't burn bridges
She burns gardens
Fruitless ones
All the planting and sowing means nothing when it's time to bloom and
nothing produces

She despises your failure to be ripe
Doesn't matter if her ground is good
She bloomed from concrete
She expects nothing less from you
You better grow
Otherwise,
She will chop you at the roots with a flaming machete
Scorching your seeds

Journeying Decisions

It's okay to stay
if it's what you want
It's okay to leave
if that's what's best
Love has no rule book
What works for one, may not be for you
It's okay to cry
Hell it's okay to mourn, just don't stay there

I Got You

Come let me hold you
I know my arms are not his
But know they are flowing in love

Come let me love you
I know my words aren't his truth
But know my "I love you" will have to do

Come let me hold you
I know your cry may not fall on his ears
But know I've cried those same fears

Come let me hold you
I know my touch could never feel as good as his
But know my hands have healed you before

Come let me hold you
I know my love may not be as good as his
But never forget I taught you, you are love
That kind of love never leaves
It never deceives
And it's the best thing since you are a part of me

Come,
Let me hold you
Let's pray, let's forgive and let's heal

Somber Rays

Depression is dank and dark
I opened the window to get some air in
The sun began to cry
He said he missed me
Show yourself from beneath your covers
Wipe your tears from your eyes
Pull back your hair
What has you so down?
Are you melancholy perhaps?
Smile my dear
Don't you know who you are?
I shine for you and you still walk in gloom
Allow me to remove the clouds you wear as a crown
You were meant to shine

Sister to Sister

I AM NOT a "bad bitch"
Although you've been led to believe it's a term of endearment,
Real women fear it
Turn ear to it
Walking away, chanting and praying our daughters didn't catch wind to
it

I will not allow you to influence or undermine everything every strong
woman has tried to teach preach and instill
No,
I will not be partaking in any hashtagging of #badbitchesmatter because
frankly,
They DON'T
I will not be quoting any Trina, Ludacris or Webbie
I'd take "BASIC" if it preserves any type of dignity

I ask,
How high does your throne rest?
Can you stretch your hand in God's plan and move mountains in plain
girls?
Or are you making Plain Jane feel like she's to blame for not being
wife'd?
Have you learned the basics?
Patience
Understanding
Loyalty
Forgiveness
Are you able to forgive yourself for being disloyal because you lack
understanding of patience?

Our treasures are not for sale my dear
Our presence alone should create excitement
and fear
No one fears a "bad bitch"
They fear strong, dedicated, educated, loving,
praying women
It forces lost boys to be become men and fathers to their children

Be an investment that is fruitful
Be an upgrade and not a play thing

Address me with some respect and come correct because I deserve it
I've earned it
Log off YouTube, Facebook, and iTunes
Be more in tune with yourself and never tune your "queen" out
You are WOMAN, and there is nothing "bad" about it

Me, Myself, and...

Good morning wonderful you
Blessed woman
Courageous flower
Whose soul shall we save today?
How many men will fall to our feet?
How many lives will we take as our hips sway left to right?
Don't they know our thoughts are facts?
We are science and religion
God and us are one
Scriptures and holy water tears
Always truth
Wonderful you
Courageous flower
Who told you, you could grow anywhere?
Sprout from anything?
Be anything?
Birth any dream?
We did, that's who

T.K.O.

Don't waste all your purpose on someone else
They may never appreciate your sweat
Save some for you baby girl,
when mornings are rough, weekends are long, and nights are
treacherous.
Stand in the mirror and affirmation yourself to CHIN UP
Lipstick your smile back, and mascara soul back into your eyes
Remember to fight for YOU,
Ali and Holyfield in high heels and backless dresses
Seductive perfumes and soft skin
Kind words and loving embraces

Let him stare at your ass as you walk away... undisputed, undefeated
and unbothered

Candy

I got that Jolly Rancher watermelon
Sweet clit
That Laffy Taffy
You can have it Now and Later so
When you are hungry why wait.. eat this
Cavities that will last just cuz I walk pass
Sweet tooth, tooth fairy
Willy Wonka, Jawbreakers and heartbreaker sweetness
And you must admit,
You need this
All over your peppermint stick!

Lips thick as molasses flows
Baby my Blow Pop so sick
It'll make you Ring Pop my shit
Savor every flavor of my Lifesaver
Sour like Lemonheads & Sour Patch Kids
Sweet like Tootsie Pops and gumdrops
See, ain't nothing sugar free about me
Baby I am original, wild berry and tropical fruit
I'm a hand full of penny candy
And you're a mouth full of Sugar Daddy
Watch it pour like Pixy Stix
Yeah I got that sweet drip
It got you rock candy hard,
We gettin' it bubble gum poppin'
I got you going Dum Dum for a taste
Of my Bubble Yum yum

I explode like Pop Rocks
So don't stop playing with my SweeTarts Sweetheart
Since I'm one Hot Tamale, you'll probably need to Take 5 to stay alive
swimming between my thighs' Milky Ways
Baby, Ruth ain't felt this good on a Payday
Ask Mike & Ike, they know what's up
I melt in your mouth and not in your hands

118

That's 100 Grand
Ya hands know it too
Blueberry, raspberry straws
I have no flaws

So let your eyes take a glimpse of my jelly beans
If you know what I mean
They'll have you screaming
Swinging from Red Vines
Even your Peeps can see I'm fine
Just don't play in my Fun Dip
But make it drip like candy paint
I'll have you sitting sideways
Puffing a pack a day on candy cigs
My hips allow good trips of deep, sweet flips, sheet grips, cuffs
Licorice whips...
I told you,
I'm Jolly Rancher watermelon, Starburst,
Gusher sweet...
You ready to eat?

Trill

Love is for pretty girls
Barefaced heavenly creatures
No earrings and messy buns
party songs with classical features
      They be symphony sweet

I be nothing like them
Bold lipstick fire mouthpiece
Gold hoops and pixie cuts
trap music with mean mug
      I be Chopped and screwed mixtape

Birthing Endless Summer

The tears stopped
I am finding my place
Staying in a dark space for too long always
Stunts growth

Sunrays,
bouncing off my chest, striking anyone or anything
in my path
My aura, light
My center, bright
Ignoring those clouds that used to follow me
No longer are they my halo
Now stepping-stones on which I elevate self
Now I know,
I've always belonged up here

Never should have tried to bury myself alive
I was sinking when I should have been floating
I am not just the dirt I was blown from
I am more than my pain
Breathing and standing in the sun
Providing and offering healing on my skin
I feel alive
I lean my head back and close my eyes
Smiling and inhaling peace
The sun smells like freedom

Sun Dragon

I am walking Oshun
Citrine crystal strong
Sun colored, ain't I
Something blinding
I am yella, ain't I

My light evoking straight, spine, like
staff holding up nations
Breast plump
Indulge in feeding or pleasing
Arms that branch understanding
Fingers that offer healing
Medicine woman
Voodoo conjuring and candle burning

Stomach scarred from stretching
and exhaling God's breath
Holy wounds surrounded my navel
Revelations and affirmations
proclaiming home in this host
Thighs thick enough to roux your existence,
gumbo your lineage
Knees that bend in prayer and pleasure
You ought not worship but grovel in awe of my reign

Feet giving foundation like platforms to reach God on,
but feel so good in your hands
Red polished toenails in mouth
Setting your words on fire
I made you dragon

I am the beast in you
Taming and unleashing you
You don't own you....
My lips do

Big Girl Panties

He requests I be woman
Unsure if he is able to stand as man and what that means,
no longer seems to matter when the topic of my 'woman' is brought up

I need to be woman,
I should feed self-confidence instead of insecurities because that's what's
really sexy
Sadly, the same thing that makes me eat
makes me want to starve
So clearly sexy is not within reach
Sometimes me is not within seek but here he is, requesting:

Be strong
Turn me on
Be soft, but don't make me
Give me head but don't be a headache
Cook and clean
Don't be mean
Give me space
Look at me in my face when I talk to you
And naw,
I don't want to talk about it!
Be ok with that, but don't be weak
You must stay, but I could walk away at anytime
Hell, it's my dime that gets us by, so be grateful
Understand that I'm the best out here, yet you, you could use a little
work
I accept you but I expect you to be better
Don't talk back
Better start giving me some slack…
I am king,
Know your place and stay there

But you want me to be woman
And if you are King,
Well then, I am Queen!
Soooo who you think you talking to?

Oh excuse me,
You must have me mistaken for one of the peasants you unwillingly grew immune to
Baby, don't you know you had to grow before you could ever see me,
Let alone step?
You couldn't even get a "Hello" from me until you learned to pursue diligently!
And since I am worth it,
Courtship is required,
Wooing is desired and recommended if
you'd like to get and keep my attention

Because see,
I am woman
Creator
Lover
Pleaser
Boy, I'll cook and clean and do it so mean…
you knew it was nice
My sugar and spice is the perfect blend
for any day's end
My heart is home
I stand strong,
Alone and by your side
Unafraid to let you lead, but ready to shine at any time, if and when necessary
Honey, understand my love is never secondary…
It's primary!
Primarily the reason you feel the need to be a part of all my seasons
See,
CAN'T NO WOMAN, WOMAN LIKE ME

Lagniappe

Something Extra

Message from Monk

Round Midnight
Trumpets blow your essence
While saxophones vibrate from the belly of heaven
On this day stay, stand tall
Upright bass
Afraid not to phrase it how you want
Never ashamed to be ahead of the beat
Behind it if need be
Sound your percussion for Miles
Drum Max
Scat us Fitzgerald and melodic energies as you toss and turn waiting for
sun to rise
Jazz,
Jazmyn,
Gardenia fragrant laughter
Billie,
Be bold in cadence
Apologize not when your Bebop happens on broken time
Groove
Jump
Play free
No orchestra
Just solo
Counting off your magic
Jaz has returned

June's Moon

Standing still in an hourglass, knowing our time is sacred
Perfect
God given
Understanding that we have the power to understand forever and we
can make that sand stop and spin
Sandcastles built with hands of steel and hearts of gold are refuge in
turmoil
We control the waves and we coast
Sailing on a crescent moon in and out of time
We are timeless
Forever standing tall for each other as we fall more and more ....in
love

Balancing on forever
We never know how love moves
It can surprise us
Scare us and shape us into the people we are today
Standing face to face,
I know I have met my match
We have called it a draw
The towel has been thrown in
You stand tall like a floor length mirror
Like secret prayers answered
Causing me to reflect
And dig and find truth
Find me
Keeping me forever young
In spirit
In space
Always playing hide and seek because you keep me guessing
Keep me laughing
How I love your laugh
Don't you know God and I talked about you?
I told him to let me grow to you
To us
Never wanting to get it right on the first try because forever means
trying

Trying to understand
Trying not to pretend
Trying to not try, and to be grateful when we do
Love, my dear, means trying and making it look effortless simply
because you are you!

Never taking back any argument
They make the good times shine
And look at us,
Two stars
Shining
And shooting
Shooting for each other's heart
Shooting for the moon because we are far beyond the now
Our love be something like ether kisses
God knew what he had done
What we had won
And can't no man tear us apart
I promise my prayers are heard every time,
How do you think we got here
Our hugs be like church
When two or more are present so is he
And he is with us always
I am with you always
Always fighting
Laughing
Shooting and shining and trying...
Always and forever

Note to Self

I am fly
Sexy
Smart
And funny as hell

I am sweet
Thoughtful
Emotional
And a great mother

I am genuine
Blessed
Creative
And I am spiritual!

I am loyal
Fiery
Feisty
And I am amazing

I am growing
Flourishing
Developing
And I am becoming who I'm supposed to be

How lucky you are to be in my space
To know me
How lucky you are if I smile at you, speak and acknowledge you
How lucky you are to be my friend,
How lucky are you to be my man,
How lucky you are to say you love me and to be loved by me.
I am a catch and never again
Will I let someone make me feel like I am not worthy
I am worth every effort
I am worth fighting for
I am worth not walking away from
And you will never regret loving me!!!

Morning Dye

Sunbeams scorch white curtains
Morning glow from last night's shadows
I awake knowing I am poetry
My freckles are guided truths
Connecting the dots of my lineage
My skin, a flavorful blend
Sweet ingredients and savory seasonings

Feeling blessed to inhale in my shadows
My mornings are always brighter
Hopeful eyes shine outward with surrendering hands high
God runs though me
His Sun beams on me
I am a poem,
I am amazing
I am awake

Portraits While I Wait

Filters filter each mood captured with lenses
A collage of wonderful
Interpret if you must, but make sure you have an eye for art
If not, you might misinform the public!
Perception can cause revolutions
Perfection is always the cause for evolution
I am a masterpiece only the third eye can see!!

HNIC

Who is really in need of urgent care,
Is it me?
Charting ailments and flulike nonsense in my sleep
Just getting to work can be a headache
Barely getting in the car and 3 people have called out

My woes go unaddressed in meetings
I am the boss
I don't have the luxury to complain
I am a problem solver
HNIC
Head Nurse in Charge
And I got a LVN that knows how to push my buttons
With any luck, she would be the next to call out but it doesn't work that
way

Paperwork on top of paperwork
Triage and discharge
Someone just called code blue
He decided to join the circus and make money off it
Jump quick,
"Get that IV started"
"Call the doctor "
Everything is STAT except my needs

They are watching
My next move could be applauded or reported and documented
But saving lives makes it all worth it
There is more to being a nurse than getting vitals and prepping you for
the doctor
We are advocates
We are listeners
Holistic approach, bedside manner and sometimes the magic touch
Superhero in scrubs

Juggling patient complaints
HIPPA regulations

Staff scheduling conflicts
I barely have time for lunch
Not everyone can get what they want

I am
Party pooper when I stop colleagues from taking photos of a patient
Hypertrichosis, werewolf syndrome but he was there for hypertension
His unique condition turned my waiting room into a three ring circus,
and although he worked in one and was used to the attention
He wasn't there for inappropriate picture taking
I shouted to a fellow nurse "Get these people out of here!" and just like
that, I'm the bad guy

I don't come to work for their approval
I come to make sure we service the community
It is our duty to help aid the public through testing, information,
patience, understanding, and using our education to educate others
I am a nurse and I am a "missioner of health!"

*Florence Nightingale Pledge 1935

Felixinese

Who said a man couldn't love you like so even if he is not your father
I have been loved by one
Spoken highly of by one
Told I could do anything I want
Had one be on butt like white on rice before
When God keeps you connected through faith, encouragement and
childhood memories, you know love is there

Will openly talk God with me, which turns into a debate simply because
he is more Old Testament than anything
Drops "I know what I'm talking about now" jewels on boyfriends and
ain't shit "Roscos"
which ones to keep
which ones to toss
Still learning how to receive that

He has been there for all of my achievements no matter how far apart
they are
He is always proud "'bout time dammit, I knew you could do it!"
"Stop bullshitin' now"
He blows no smoke

When he gives me sound advice in the most outlandish, funny way off
the top of his head that only he knows the meaning of, but resonates
with my soul
I find myself laughing at him always "kicking but not too high"
He don't mind if I like it or you don't, that's just how it is
He has given me the keys to life over a barbecue grill
Or cigars and brown liquor once old enough, but never too old to be told
about myself

He loves tenderly with understanding
Patriarch Abraham
Dedicated believer Daniel
He is thick tongue in advice
His words are gravy

Making sure to keep a biscuit on me to sop up every drop
Aware that I will be starving even after he is gone
He has a lifetime of lessons to serve even when I'm not hungry
He makes me take a doggy bag

Proud to say I have been loved by a man that isn't my father, I thank you
for stepping up
Barefoot, Stacy Adams or sandals
You showed me why feet are so important
You are ground in love and family
I am thankful to be one of the women loved by him

Mèsi Chèr

*First and foremost I want to thank God.
Thank you for choosing me and using me. Father, your sense of humor is beyond my understanding and we got some thangs to go over when we come face-to-face, spirit-to-spirit. All glory goes to you, Lord.

*Ma, thank you for always being my rock. Thank you for birthing me and keeping me swaddled in strength and unconditional promise. You are the best representation of woman and mother I've ever known. I wouldn't be anything without your love and support. Thank you for always reminding me that I am powerful and gifted. Thank you for raising me to be free... you my girl!!!

*Jayla, baby girl, you are the best thing that ever happened to me. You make me better, you make me brave, you make me woman. I continuously pray you write your story in the sky. You are a warrior JayBird... mommy loves you and I will always have your back.

*To my family and friends, thank you for always believing me and reminding me of my goodness. I find comfort knowing that no matter how far we may drift apart in our own lives, family and true friendship is always home and always love.

*To World Stage Press and staff, thank you for supporting, creating, celebrating and publishing my words. Hiram Sims, Nadia Hunter Bey, Camari Carter, and G.T. Foster, thank you for believing I had a story worth telling and reading. Undeniable Ink, you are wonderful energy and you bring thoughts to color.

*To my CLIck, season 3, alumni, and current writers...you make me push my pen. I'm so grateful to be in the wonderfulness that is you. Keep writing, keep shaming the devil, and keeping telling it like is (in my Aaron Neville voice)! You all have magic in your heads, thank you for sharing your spells. Jaha Zainabu, it is truly a blessing to be in your

137

presence weekly as I digest what it truly means to be a writer.

*To the co-founders Billy Higgins and Kamau Daaood of The World Stage Performance Gallery in Leimert Park, much appreciation to your vision and groundbreaking influence in my world of poetry as well as many others's. Thank you V. Kali and Conney Williams for all of your hard work to keep the Anasi Writers Workshop going and requiring artists to come to the stage with their best work. Artists like Peter J Harris, Michael Datcher, Dee Black, El Rivera and many others, thank you for setting the tone, and for the "no bullshit" sign that is visible every Wednesday night.

*To all the open mic spots and venues that give people like me the space and freedom to share our stories, you are the bomb. A special thank you to O'Shea Kwa Luja (Food4Thot) and Melanie S. Luja (Queen Socks) for Still Waters and Thursday Night Vibes at Vibrations in Inglewood, CA. For the blessed energy, griot knowledge that was available in the truthbrary, the soul quenching words, and teas that can heal just about anything, I am forever thankful. You were my church when I had heavy feelings, was broken hearted, and especially when everything was all right. You help cultivate land where poems and goodness grow. #JessLight. To my FAMILY, The Last Sunday in Culver City, CA at the U.S.V.A.A, thank you for your always supportive connection. You have welcomed me and my tribe, and so many others like mine. You gave me the space to be free; thank you to J. W. Gardner and Bobby Strahan. Lady Basco and Beau Siea at Our Mic, y'all are giving us artists something that's never been done. Thank you for sharing your experiences and knowledge of the arts while helping us find the tools to demolish boundaries in our art and ourselves. #youshineIshine. A huge shout out to venues like Da Poetry Lounge, A Mic and Dim Lights, Shades of Afrika, Tuesday Night Project, Flight School, and many other amazing spaces that I don't have the space to name. I appreciate your love and dedication to the people and the arts. It takes a village and we are one voice of many truths.

*To the management team Wilbert Ho, Cathy Bell, Beatrisa Bannister, and the staff at LAC+USC, I just want to say thank you for your never ending encouragement and understanding with the journey and creation of this book. Your support is mind-blowing, bless all of you.

*To Maya Angelou, Langston Hughes, Nina Simone, UGK, Jill Scott, Sam Cooke, Nikki Giovanni, Fats Domino, T-Lou and Lauryn Hill, thank you for dwelling in my bones.

*To the women who have "sister fire circled" me in hugs, laughs and tears, in "hell yes," in affirmation and in queen,
-Reverida "da river woman"
-Nadia Hunter Bey
-Michelle Williams
-Ieshya Parker
-Camari Carter
-Lauren Delay
-Ramona Turner
-Genesia Rose
-October Blue
You ladies continuously remind me to adjust my crown and own my crazy. You're always understanding and trusting in the power of growth and doing my own work. I couldn't woman with all this cayenne if it weren't for your constant requests to walk in my fire. I love you in a place that only you and God have access to.

*To the men that have supported and encouraged me in woman, in pen, in love and in art
-Derek Brown
-Eternal Mind
-Hiram Sims
-Akoldpiece
-C-Bone Jones
-George McDonald
-Kauhmel
-Sipho N'Jedi
-Darryl Lewis
-My dad Ben Roque (RIP)
-Uncle Felix
-Dominique Clifton
-Uncle Al Long (RIP)
Words aren't enough to express the magnitude of how honored I am to have your protective love and strength guarding the gates of my woman.

*Last but certainly not least Cher, I want to thank the wonderful individual that is you, holding this book and reading these words. Thank you for being a supporter of this work and of me. I welcome you into my world and my tribe! We shonuff people now, sho'ya right... thank you!!

Jessica Gallion was born in Shreveport, Louisiana and raised in Los Angeles where pen and poetry became her best friend. Inspired by the works of Maya Angelou and Langston Hughes, she decided that she too had a story to tell. She is a nomad for the art, never fitting into a particular place, therefore making space for herself wherever her voice is needed. She writes for the misunderstood, the hurt and abused — she writes for you. As a single mother, a creole woman, and a woman who knows the fire and flaws of life, she uses her pen to shine light in dark places. She has performed at Vibrations, The World Stage, Flight School, and many other venues around Los Angeles. Jessica is the 2016 champion of the Spoken Word Voices Heard poetry slam, was one of the only two women features on the A Few Good Men Tour, and a feature at Equinox at The Creative House and The Last Sunday at U.S.V.A.A. She is also a season 3 graduate of the Community Literature Initiative and a published author with World Stage Press.

To the monsters that question who, what and why we are. The ones in the world and the ones in our head, hush up... I'm busy.

141

Made in the USA
San Bernardino, CA
10 February 2018